Sharing is Healing

A Holocaust Survivor's Story

2nd Edition

Noémi Bán

Holocaust Educational Publications
922 38th Street
Bellingham, WA 98229-3158
http://SharingIsHealing.com
SharingIsHealing@comcast.net

ISBN 0-9772130-0-5

This book is dedicated to the memories
of my dear ones:
my grandmother Nina,
my mother Juliska,
my sister Erzsébet,
and my brother Gábor.
Their lives ended in Auschwitz.

It is also dedicated to the memory
of my dear husband Earnest.
His love helped me realize that sharing is healing.

"*Sharing is Healing* is a well-written, extremely moving book… It is deliberately written in a simple style so a child can understand it, yet its very simplicity makes its message all the more chilling. The atrocities of the Nazi regime are never sensationalized, yet they are quite clear and horrifying. The events of the Holocaust, and the specific experiences of Ms. Ban, are made plain enough for even young children to understand."

—Writer's Digest

"Seldom does a book have such a powerful message as *Sharing is Healing*… The straight forward writing style make this a must read book for readers of all ages even though it is written at a sixth grade level… I would strongly recommend this book to your students in a college reading class, because of the high interest level and the life story that Noemi Ban shares with the readers."

—The Journal of College Literacy and Learning

Table of Contents

Introduction to Noémi's Story

by Ray Wolpow

Sharing is Healing is a book written by Noémi Ban. She survived the Holocaust. Mrs. Ban survived the ghetto, the cattle cars and Auschwitz. Many members of her family were killed in the camps. She suffered there. But Noémi did not write this book to teach you the facts of the Holocaust. It is her story of hope. It is a Holocaust survivor's gift of love and understanding.

How this Book is a Gift

A gift is something special, something chosen for you. It is given because the giver wants you to have it. Sharing is Healing is a gift for you from Noémi.

The events in this book show how cruel people can be to each other. Telling about these terrible things is not Noémi's gift. Her gift for you is her story. In her story Noémi tells how she kept hope alive. She shares how she has never given up. She shows the value of friendship. She shares about doing the right thing even when others do not. She shows how sharing is healing. The hope and love in her story is Noémi's gift to you.

Love is Healing

This Holocaust survivor's story is also about the power of love over hate. There is so much hate in the world. Even a little hate is dangerous. Hate can be an excuse to be cruel to others. Feeling hate can be a way to think that you are better than someone else. Noémi knows. She suffered in Auschwitz.

Hate hurts but love heals. Love is respectful. Love has **sympathy**[1]. Love is caring. Love is what brings us back together when we have been hurt. Love is what reminds us that we are all human beings.

As you read this book listen to the way that Noémi talks about people. She doesn't want to be a prisoner of her own hate. She wants to fill her life with love and friendship.

Understanding Takes More Than Words.

Sharing is Healing is also a gift of understanding. Perhaps you have had bad things happen in your life? Perhaps you have had a loved one die. Or perhaps someone you know has had to suffer great pain. Or, perhaps something awful happened to you. If so, then you know that words can't always describe what you feel. Yes, we can learn the facts. But the facts don't tell the whole story. Understanding takes more than words.

Noémi is a good listener. She knows what it is like to suffer. She was starved and mistreated. Nearly her entire family was killed. For those who have had tough times, Noémi is like a treasure chest of hope. Noémi understands. She is a survivor.

Listening Can Also Be Healing

The title of this book is Sharing is Healing. As you read Noémi's words you will discover why it heals to share. But as you read you might also discover that it heals you when you listen. Maybe you will remember a time when you were very sad.

---

[1] *Sym-path-y:* Sympathy is trying to understand or share the feelings of another person. When you feel sympathy, what affects someone else also affects you.

Listening to Noémi's hope may help you feel hope too. I know. I am the one who has helped Noémi write down her story. I have watched and listened many times. A part of me feels stronger each time I listen.

In 1995 I traveled with Noémi to Auschwitz. This was the first time she had been back to this place where terrible things happened to her and her loved ones. (You can read about this in chapter 6.) I listened and I cried. When we returned home, a part of me felt stronger.

A Few Words About How This Book is Written

Noémi wrote this book in simple language. Sentences are kept short. Bolded subheadings divide parts of the chapter so that the ideas will be easier to understand. Before reading each chapter you may want to take time to read each of the bolded subheadings. You may also want to look at the words that are in **bold face**. If you don't know the meaning of one of these words go to the bottom of that page. Vocabulary meanings are written there.

Why This Book is Written this Way

Noémi is an award-winning 6th grade teacher. She could have easily written this book with longer sentences. But she knows better. Long sentences would not make her story any easier to understand.

Instead, Noémi wrote this book thinking of the many students that she has taught. Some of them were good readers. Others were learning how to read better. Noémi wanted to make sure that all students could read it.

Whether you are a strong reader or not, please take time to read this book. Accept Noémi's gift of love and understanding. Listen with an open heart. A part of you may become stronger too.

Have You Ever Studied about the Holocaust?

Did you say "yes"? Then you know that the Holocaust was a very cruel time. You know the Holocaust took place during World War II. You know who the Nazis were. You know about Adolph Hitler. You know about ghettos, cattle cars, concentration camps, and forced labor. You know the Nazis killed nearly 6 million Jews. You know they killed millions of others too. You know about gas chambers, smoke, and ash.

Did you say "no"? Then this book may be hard for you to understand. If you don't know about the Holocaust, please do one thing before reading this book. Please talk to your teacher or to somebody else who knows. Get him or her to help you learn about the terrible things that happened to millions of people. That way this book won't shock you. Get him or her to explain what life was like in Europe in the 1930's. Get him or her to show you a map of the area. That way you will know where Hungary, Poland and Germany are. This will help you to picture the events in the book. It will also help you to know where and why some things in this book were happening.

Sharing is Healing

by Noémi Ban
with Ray Wolpow

Chapter One:
The Nazis Come to our Town

Hitler² became the leader of Germany in 1933. From then on, Jewish people were in danger. Hitler told the Germans that they should get rid of the Jews. In his mind, Jews caused bad things to happen to Germany. Hitler told people that the Jews were like insects and rats. He said the Jews even poisoned the air when they breathed. Hitler had so much hate in his heart.

In 1939, World War II broke out. Hitler's army took over one country after the other. We in *Hungary³* knew about the war. We hoped that we would not be involved. But, Hitler's armies were winning. We hoped they would lose soon. But, on March 19, 1944 Hitler's *SS⁴* troops took over Hungary. We were so afraid! My little sister ran home from school. She was crying. She asked, "Will those soldiers kill us?" Our family was Jewish. We knew bad things had happened to the Jews in Germany.

---

² *Hit-ler:* Adolf Hitler was known as "Der Führer." He was born in 1889 and died in 1945. He started the German Nazi Party. He was also the chancellor of the Third Reich (1933-1945). His beliefs were written into his book Mein Kampf. He became very popular in Germany. After 1934 he ruled as an absolute dictator. Hitler's policies resulted in the invasion of Poland in 1939 and World War II. He is known for the killing of millions of people, especially European Jews.

³ *Hun-ga-ry:* A country in Europe. People who live there are called Hungarians. There are 10 million Hungarians.

⁴ *SS:* This is an abbreviation for the German word Schutzstaffel. Schutzstaffel means "Defense Corps." The SS was a military group. The SS had two main purposes: 1) to protect Hitler and the other important Nazis. 2) To control the ghettos and concentration camps. Its members wore skull and crossbones on their hats. They also wore lightning bolts on their lapels.

What Would Happen to Us?

We had fear in our hearts. What would happen to us? We didn't have to wait long to find out. Members of the **Arrow Cross**[5] (Hungarian **Nazis**[6]) came to our house. They told us to stand in our backyard. They told us that in a few days large posters would be glued onto the walls outside the houses. We had to read and obey them. On them were the "Jewish Laws."

A yellow Star of David badge bearing the German word 'Jude' (Jew). [Photograph #N00277 from the U.S. Holocaust Memorial Museum] (Used with Permission)

The first law told us to wear the yellow star. We had to wear it whenever we went outside. Where should we get those yellow stars? The Arrow Cross told us. We had to march to the store. Soldiers were all around us. We had to use our own money to buy yellow stars. We had to sew one onto each piece of clothing we had on.

Imagine how embarrassed we were when we had to go outside. People looked at us wherever we went. We knew in our hearts that something much more terrible would soon come.

---

[5] **Ar-row Cross:** The Hungarian Nazi party. These Hungarians were on Hitler's side. When the Nazi army came into Hungary, the Arrow Cross welcomed them with open arms.

[6] **Na-zi:** A member of the National Socialist German Workers' Party. This party was started in Germany in 1919 and brought to power in 1933 under Adolf Hitler.

Crowded into a Ghetto

Two days later came the next order. The order said: "All Jews have to live in the ghetto!" What is a **ghetto**[7]? A ghetto is a small location where many people are crowded together. The Nazis wanted us to all be in one small part of the city. That way they were able to watch us. There were Jewish families in different parts of the city. They had to move to houses in the ghetto. In the ghetto, we became prisoners. Our house was already in the ghetto. So on that day we became prisoners in our own home.

One day, eight more families moved into our house. They didn't want to. They were told they had to leave their homes. They had to move to the ghetto. We did not have a large enough house for so many people. We also did not have enough food for them all. People slept in the hallway.

If somebody had to go to the bathroom, they had to stand in line. Nine families lived in our one small house.

Our house was on the **borderline**[8] of the ghetto. In front of our house was a sidewalk. In front of the sidewalk was the street for trucks and buses. But, we were not allowed to go out our front door. That is because this was the "free" part of our city. We had to stay on the ghetto side.

---

[7] **Ghetto:** A part of a city chosen by the Nazis for Jews. Too many people lived in this small part of the city.

[8] **Bor-der-line:** A boundary. This was the line that separated the ghetto from the rest of the city. Sometimes there was a wall built on the borderline. Sometimes it was a sidewalk or a street. Other times the line was imaginary. However, being shot or punished for going on the wrong side of the borderline was not imaginary.

3

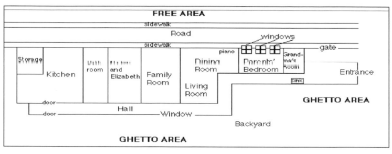

This is a drawing of the floor plan of Noémi's house.

From our front windows, we could see the free side. But we could not go there. We were prisoners. We couldn't even say hello to the people on the free side. These people were our neighbors. But because of the ghetto, they became strangers. The Hungarian Nazis told us we could not go out our front gate. We obeyed out of fear for our lives.

Life Changes More and More

It felt like dark clouds were gathering above us. Here is the story of one sad day. This day made me realize how life was changing. It also made me realize how much power the Nazis had over us.

Our family had a dearly loved piano. It was made with dark wood. My mother had **crocheted** [9] a cover, out of yarn to put on top. Our piano looked and sounded great. Most important, our piano gave us special memories.

I started taking piano lessons when I was five. I practiced almost every day for 14 years. I learned how to play wonderful music. My father played the violin. Sometimes we would play together. My mother listened while we played. You can see why I loved this piano so much.

---

[9] **Cro-chet**: A kind of needlework. A large needle with a big hook on the end is used to knit and weave yarn. Crochet is often used to make hats, covers and decorations.

Noémi's mom, Noémi (age 12), her sister Elizabeth (age 4), and Noémi's Father

One day we heard a loud knock at our front door. We looked at each other with fear. Who was coming now? What did they want? My father opened the door. Four strong men marched in. They were wearing worker's clothes. They were complete strangers.

One of them spoke. "We have come to take away your piano." They had no papers. They had no orders. They were just here to take our piano. My father asked them, "Where are you taking our piano?" With hate and anger they answered, "We are making room for the many people in your house." They took it out the front door to the free side. As they walked out I cried. I had the feeling that somebody died. Little did I know there would soon be other reasons to cry.

A few days later came another order. Every man between 18 and 55 years old had to report to "***work service.***[10]"

---

[10] **Work ser-vice:** Because German men were in the army, extra workers were needed. These workers sometimes worked in factories. Other times they dug ditches or carried supplies. Those forced to do "work service" were not paid for their work. That is why "work service" is also called slave labor or forced labor.

What was "work service?" We didn't know. My father, 48 years old, had to go. Would he be back? We didn't know. Who would protect us? We didn't know. I remember watching him pack his backpack. As my mom helped him she was crying. The next morning my father left with tears in his eyes. First he blessed us, "God bless you and save you," he said. Then he left.

All of us were crying. Our hearts were broken. That whole day and into the night my mother kept crying. I was also very sad. But I tried to calm down my mom. I told her, "Please don't cry. Maybe soon you will see him again."

She shook her head and said, "Noémi, I have a terrible feeling that I will never see him again." I am sorry to tell you that my mom was right. They never met again. Never!

We Do Our Best To Keep Hope Alive

Noémi's Grandma

In the ghetto, who was left behind? There were only old grandpas and grandmas, small boys and girls, young mothers and young girls. The same was true for our family. Our family was now only five people. First I will tell you about my dear grandma. She was a small woman with a loving smile. Soon she would be eighty years old. She was a great cook. She baked delicious cookies and had a lovely voice. We often asked her to sing for us. Her room always smelled so good. This was because of what she did during the winter. Grandma put apple-peel on top of her wood stove. I can still remember the wonderful smell.

My dear mom was 43 years old. She loved to read and do needlework. She also loved to write letters to her family. When I was little she took me to the library. My dear mom was my best friend. She trusted me. There was nothing we couldn't talk about. She let me read books for older children. Then we would talk about them. My mother taught me to love books. She also taught me to read my favorite books over and over again.

My sister, Elizabeth, was tall, skinny and very smart. I was nine years older than her.

When something happened to Elizabeth she would turn to me. I would be the one with an answer. I would help.

My baby brother's name was Gábor. He had shiny black hair and black eyes. He didn't cry a lot. He was a tiny baby, only 6 months old. But, when he cried he had a very strong voice. I have no pictures to

Elizabeth, age 12

show you of Gábor. Soon you will understand why.

We had less and less food. We missed my father. The fear in our hearts was growing. What would happen to us? We did our best to keep going. We did our best to keep hope in our hearts.

Nailing a Coffin?

One day men came again. They came from the free side. They brought boards, nails and hammer. They did not knock on the door. We looked out the window. We watched them, but not for long. They started to nail up boards. The boards covered the windows. We were no longer able to see the free world. Now we really felt like prisoners. We couldn't even look out our own window. One person in our house started to cry. She said, "I feel like I am in my own coffin. These men are nailing the lid closed on me." I felt a chill running through me. Terrible fear and concern were growing more and more.

Picture by Nicholas Wetter, Lakeside High School ('02), Plummer, Idaho (Used with Permission)

Why I Didn't Run and Hide

After my father had to leave I had a chance to escape. In the ghetto there were some young men. They didn't have to go to "work service." This was because they were under 18.

I met one of these young men. He and his friends had worked out a plan. They had a secret printing machine. They could use it to help Jewish girls to escape the ghetto. This is how they did it: They made false *ID[11]* papers. On these papers they could say we were a different religion. This man and his friends would then help us escape to *Budapest[12]*. When we got there we would pretend we were not Jewish. Here non-Jews would hide us.

Today these non-Jews are called *righteous gentiles[13]*. They risked their lives to save ours. They would say that we were their maids. They would also mislead the Nazis to protect us.

Back in the ghetto I talked to the young man. He told me about this plan. He told me about the printing machine. He told me about the righteous gentiles. He offered to help me to escape. This was a hard decision. Here is the reason why:

Six months before the Nazis came to Hungary my mother gave birth to my little brother. It was a hard

---

[11] *ID:* Identification papers. These are the papers we used to prove who we were. In America one might use a driver's license as an ID.

[12] *Bu-da-pest:* The capital of Hungary. It is also the largest city in Hungary.

[13] *Right-eous Gen-tiles:* Brave non-Jews who risked their lives to save Jews. Each word here has a meaning. Righteous means they were doing what was right. They did what was right even though they were risking their lives. Gentile is a word that Jews use to describe those who are not Jewish.

labor. Then there was more bad news. My mother had a **blood clot**[14] in her leg. In 1944 there was no medicine for blood clots. The doctors said my mother had to stay in bed. If she didn't, the blood clot might move. If the clot moved to her heart, or her lungs, or her brain, she would die. Now you understand why, for six months, my mother had to be in bed. I helped out until it was safe for her to move around.

Then my dad was sent to the "work service." My grandma was old and not in good health. My mother still had bandages on her leg. My sister was only 12 years old. I was healthy and strong. They all loved me. They also needed me. How could they manage without my dad and without me? I told the man I was grateful that he wanted to help me. "Thank you," I said, "but I will stay here. I cannot leave my dear family." Little did I know what would happen next.

---

[14] **Blood clot:** A medical condition. Sometimes blood cells get clogged. This blocks the flow of blood in an artery or vein. This is a dangerous condition. If a blood clot gets into the heart or lungs, a person can die. Today there is medicine to unclog this problem. In the days when Noémi's mother was alive, there was no such medicine.

Chapter Two:
From the Brick Factory, to the Cattle Car, to Auschwitz

Three long months went by. There was less and less food to eat. People were nervous and afraid. We all missed our fathers, brothers and uncles.

One day a new law came. It told us that on the next day everybody in the ghetto had to line up in their backyards. The soldiers even told us what to pack. Take "one small pillow, one bed sheet, one small package of dry food, no valuables, and last, one change of underwear!" Where are we going? Why do we need only one change of underwear? We should have asked these questions. But we didn't ask because we were so afraid!

Marching to the Brick Factory

We packed and the next day we all lined up. We all wore the yellow star. We had to march through the city. People were lining up on the streets watching us. Some people stared. Others yelled unkind things. We were embarrassed and afraid. We walked for a long time.

Finally we arrived at a brick factory. Here we saw hundreds and hundreds of people. Some were our neighbors. Others were from the countryside. With guns pointed at us, we went in. We had to climb up to the second floor on the ladders. As I was climbing on the ladder a soldier used his **bayonet**[15] to push me up.

---

[15] *Bayonet*: A large blade that is attached to the barrel of a rifle. Soldiers can then use the point of the rifle to poke or stab others.

He poked me a long time ago, but I am still able to point to the spot on my back where it hurt.

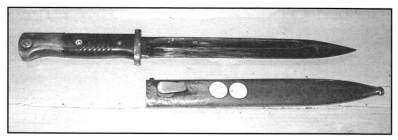

Photograph of a Hungarian bayonet by C. Alan Russell (Used with permission)

The second floor was only dirt and walls. Here we slept. We used the pillow and bed sheet we had packed. Everything: water, food, and bathroom were down below. My dear mother and my old grandma had to climb up and down the ladders. Life was hard. We got very little food. After ten days we felt dirty; we were hungry and always full of fear. Fear and dread filled our hearts. What will happen to us?

At last, an order came to line up. We were almost "happy" that we are leaving that very bad place. We had hopes. We hoped that maybe they were sending us to some place better. A human being always hopes for the best. It didn't get better. Our situation only got worse.

SS Soldiers and Cattle Cars

The Hungarian Nazis lead us to the railroad yard of the factory. Here they gave us over to the waiting SS soldiers. We were terrified when we saw them. Behind the SS soldiers was a long, long train made of ***cattle cars[16]***.

---

[16] ***Cat-tle Car:*** These are railroad cars. They are sometimes called boxcars. Prisoners were crowded into the cattle cars. Then the doors were locked from the outside. The Hungarian cattle cars were 26.8 feet in length and 7.2 feet in width. There is a cattle car on display at the United States Holocaust Memorial Museum.

These cattle cars were small. 85 of us were crowded into the cattle car.

We were all inside. The SS yelled, "Put the packages in the center of the car and sit down!" How could we do this? There wasn't even enough room to stand! He yelled and we obeyed. We sat on the floor. We sat on each other. My mother held Gábor so he wouldn't get crushed. I protected my sister.

Two Buckets

I looked around. There were two tiny windows on each side of the cattle car. And at the two ends were two empty buckets.

I wanted to know what they were for. I asked a SS guard. We were not allowed to talk to the SS. But I still asked. It was dangerous to do this but I wanted to know. Thinking back now, maybe one reason that I survived was that I asked questions. Even when it was dangerous, I asked questions. I was a human being not a number!

To my question the guard gave his answer. One of each bucket on each side would have fresh water for us to drink. The other two were for *sanitary purposes*[17]. Yes, these buckets were to be the bathroom for 85 people! It was horrible! People were embarrassed to use it at first. Later we had to. The SS locked the door from the outside and the train slowly started to move…

---

[17] *San-i-tar-y pur-pos-es*: Sanitary has to do with keeping clean. One goes to the bathroom to wash. But one also goes to the bathroom to pee or poop. Noemi tells us that one bucket of water was for drinking. The other bucket was for peeing or pooping.

Disgusting Odor

As a young person I didn't know "smell" had a "memory." Now I know. Every time I talk about my time in the cattle car I can smell that stench. Excuse me for saying that. It was the end of June. It was hot. There was no cover on the bucket.

Soon the bucket was full. When the train jerked human waste spilled onto the floor. Even now as I am writing this, I "smell" that disgusting odor. The heat, the crowding, and the smell made many people, mostly the old ones, faint.

Inside the cattle car we were tired and scared. We were troubled and crowded. The little babies, among them was my little brother, crying. Others, babies, were beyond crying. They were screaming. Maybe their little stomachs hurt. The school age children, your age, asked "normal" questions. Where are we going? Where is my bed? What is for dinner? My sister was so scared she was grabbing my hand.

Hour after hour she wouldn't let go. They turned to their mothers for answers. They turned to their older sisters for answers. But everyone in the car was afraid. We had no answers.

My Grandma's Candleholder

The old ones, among them my grandma, had nightmares. People screamed all night long. Some people fainted. One day my grandma started to shout, "It is not yours, it is mine. Nobody can take it away from me." I looked at her. I was worried. What had happened to my dear

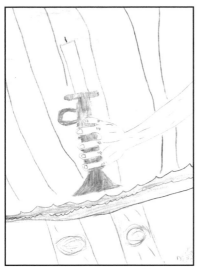

Picture by Tiana Oshiro, 6ᵗʰ grade ('02), Acme Elementary School, Acme, Washington (Used with permission)

grandma? She had nothing in her hands. I tried to calm her, "What Grandma? What do they want to take?"

All of a sudden, she bent down and from under three layers of skirts, she pulled out a heavy silver candleholder. She said, "I told you I have it, nobody can take it away from me." The noise in the cattle car stopped all at once. Why? Because everybody remembered what the SS had said.

We should not, could not, take any valuables with us. If they find this candleholder, punishment will follow. First, I didn't know what to do. Then I gave her a big hug and pried her fingers away from the candleholder. I tucked it away in my package. My package had underwear and formula for my baby brother. Then I helped her sit down. By this time my dear grandma was crying.

Why Grandma Took Such a Great Risk

We were in even greater danger. I was scared. I started thinking. Why, did my sweet grandma bring this valuable candleholder with her? She heard, as we all did, what the SS said. I kept thinking. Finally, I understood.

The candleholder was valuable because it was made of silver. But this was not the reason she had them. In our religion we light candles every Friday night. It was the

15

one we always used. The candleholder she hid under her skirts had been used for many generations. Using it to light candles was an important part of being a Jewish family.

She couldn't; wouldn't, depart from her candleholder, no matter what the SS said. I loved and respected her even more for her courage.

We Finally Arrive

We traveled 8 days. When the train finally stopped at a station I looked out a small window and I saw the name, **Auschwitz**[18]. I really didn't know where we were.

Picture by Jonathan Escalera, 7th grade ('02), Manson Secondary School, Manson, Washington (Used with permission)

I had never heard of Auschwitz. Now I know. But at the time I was just glad that the train ride was over. Living in the cattle car had been so terrible we just wanted to get out.

---

[18]*Ausch-witz*: This was the Nazi's largest death camp. It was built near Cracow, Poland. It covered more than forty square kilometers. Millions died there, mostly Jews.

16

After a long delay the train pulled into its final stop. The cattle car door opened.

Polish men in prisoner outfits were waiting for us. One man told us to get out of the cattle car. He told us to leave everything behind. Before I got out I asked the man if I could take the package with my little brother's diaper and formula. He didn't answer at first. I pleaded with him, "What will happen if my baby brother gets no food to eat?"

"How many in your family?" he asked. I told him. The prisoner in the striped outfit just said, in German, *"Schade"*[19]. This means "I'm sorry." I still remember his face. He was really sorry. But I did not yet know why.

To the Left or to the Right?

All of us were very tired. We thought things had to get better. SS soldiers with guns, bayonets and fierce dogs made us line up in pairs. I was standing with my mother who had my little brother in her arms. Behind us was my 12 year-old sister with my grandma. Poor Grandma could hardly stand.

It was a very long line and we had to move ahead, slowly, slowly we got closer to something or somebody. I couldn't see which, only I noticed that the top of the line is dividing, but I didn't know why.

Slowly, slowly we got to the top of the line where I noticed a *pedestal*[20] and on it a SS soldier in his shiny uniform. He was wearing white gloves. I could see a horsewhip in his hand. He was moving it right, left, right,

---

[19]*Scha-de*: The German word for "sorry," "too bad," or "a pity."

[20]*Pe-des-tal*: A small platform. This platform allows the person standing on it to be higher than everyone else. The SS officer stood on this platform and looked down on the prisoners. From this place up high he made the life and death selections.

Picture by Claire Smith, 6th grade ('02), Acme Elementary School, Acme, Washington (Used with permission)

right and left. As a result of his movement, some people were going one way and some the other.

As we got closer, my mother put my baby brother behind her coat. I was only able to see the shining black hair on the top of his head. My little sister was holding my hand. My grandma was there, but only in body. She was in a daze, out of her senses.

We were standing in front of the Nazi soldier.

18

Noémi's mother

He looked at us. With fear in our hearts we looked at him. The SS soldier raised the horsewhip and signaled my grandma, my mother, my sister and my little brother to his left. Another look at me and he sent me to his right. It took not more than a few seconds and I was separated from my dear ones. We couldn't talk to each other. But when I looked back I did see my dear mother bending towards me with my little brother in her arms. Then I saw her eyes, her beautiful loving eyes. Those eyes "told me, "I love you, take care"! This was the last time I ever saw them! I never saw them again.

Chapter Three

Life in the Death Camp

I was with the group signaled to the right. My dear ones were somewhere else. Everything happened so fast. I was with hundreds of people but I felt alone. Guards yelled and German shepherd dogs barked. Soon we were pushed into a huge room. Woman guards ordered us to undress. We were to hold our shoes. "Remember where you put your clothes," they yelled. We did as we were told. But my heart was broken. I missed my dear ones. I looked at the other prisoners. The sadness in their faces told me that they too were heartbroken.

Mountains of Hair

Soon we were in another room. We were told our hair would be shaved. While I was waiting for my turn I looked around. In the next room were mountains of human hair. There was one mountain of brown hair, another of black hair, and yet another of red hair. All this hair came from the prisoners. There was so much of it. The hair was piled up two times as tall as I was. (I am 5 feet, 4 inches tall.) Hair went from the floor up to the ceiling.

My whole body started to shake. I wanted to ask someone about the hair in the other room. But there was nobody to ask. My turn came. My head was shaved bare. The top of my head looked like the palm of my hand. I looked around at the other prisoners. We all looked the same. We were bald and frightened. Sisters, relatives, and friends screamed out names. They

20

couldn't find each other. Without their hair and without their clothes, we all looked the same.

Picture by Mary Morgan Vegdahl-Crowell, 7th grade ('02), Manson Secondary School, Manson, Washington (Used with permission)

The Shower Room

As soon as the shaving was done we were pushed into another room. Here we noticed showerheads high above on the ceiling. But there was nothing to turn on the showers. There was no soap. We waited a long time. The fear in us "said" that this could be the end. Finally, the guards turned on the shower from the outside. Cold water came out.

After showering we had to stand there. We were wet. We were still holding our shoes. And our shoes were wet. We had no towels, no clothes. What would happen now?!?

We were told to line up. The women guards told

us to march. We did as we were told. As we passed the guards they threw dresses up in the air. These were old dresses. We had to catch them and wear them. Whatever you caught was what you had to wear. Some tall women got small dresses. The "lucky" ones were the small women who got larger dresses. What about our regular clothes? Didn't they tell us to remember where we put them?

The Barracks

If I close my eyes I can still see this terrible place. I see gray, so much gray. I see gray gravel and gray *barracks*[21]. I see gray *barbed wire*[22] fences. I see row after row of barracks. Between the barracks are watchtowers. In the watchtowers are guards with guns in their hands. We were so frightened. They told us to march.

The guards told us to stop in front of a barrack. We were informed that this was our barrack. We were told that we were only to sleep in it. The rest of the time we were to be outside. We were to be outside in rain or shine.

We would be outside from morning until night. Our barracks, and all the others had six rooms in it. 100 people were crowded into each room. Do some fast arithmetic. Each barrack had 600 prisoners!

The barracks had no bathroom. Instead there was a *latrine*[23] outside. The latrine was a big ditch. Above the ditch were boards. The boards had small

---

[21] *Bar-racks:* The long buildings where prisoners had to sleep.

[22] *Barbed wire:* Twisted strands of fence wire with barbs at regular intervals.

[23] *La-trine:* Usually a bathroom in a separate building. In this case, a big ditch.

holes to sit over. There was no running water. Can you imagine? The stench was disgusting. Our latrine was used by hundreds of prisoners every day.

At night we were so crowded that there was no room to move. We slept on the wood floor. If someone had to go to the latrine they had to find their way in the dark. We couldn't see where we were stepping. So when we walked we would step on somebody's head, or stomach, or face. Can you imagine how this felt? We never had a quiet night. Someone was always stepped on. Someone was always yelling or crying.

Picture by Amy Holloway, Mount Vernon High School ('02), Mount Vernon, Washington (Used with permission)

The Meaning of Hunger

Early every morning we had to march out to the campground. Here we got our breakfast. It was the same breakfast every day. We were given one cup of brown water. The SS called that brown water our coffee. We were given one slice of bread. Our dinner was the same. One cup of coffee and one slice of bread. We were always very hungry.

You may notice that I haven't yet mentioned lunch. I had my reason. For lunch we had to line up in a column of five. The guards brought out a big pot of soup.

They put the pot on a small table. They then took out a tin bowl. Into the bowl they put some soup.

The next part is rather gross. The soup did not smell like food. It smelled bitter and spoiled. The soup was a dark liquid with bits of rotten vegetable in it. There was also sand and pebbles in the soup.

The first person in our line got to take a small drink from the bowl. Then she had to hand the bowl to the next person. The next person had to take her drink. She would then hand it to the next person, and so on.

The first time I saw this I refused to drink from the bowl. So did some other people. We said we didn't want any of this soup. The SS guards heard what we said. They came closer and yelled, "You'd better drink the soup! You'd better learn that in this camp there is no such thing as 'NO.' You had better do what you are told, or else!"

It was not hard to figure out what they meant by "or else." I didn't want to be killed. I wanted to stay alive. So, after that I drank the bad-smelling soup. Later people got sick. Many people got pus filled sores in and on their mouths. They got the bowl before I did. Still I had to drink after them!

Each day this is what we had to eat. We had two slices of bread. We had two cups of coffee, and one sip of soup.

The Meaning of Thirst

In this place called Auschwitz we had no running water. Sometimes we used our coffee to wash our faces. Once in a while the guards brought in drinking water. They brought this water in a tank. The tank was on the back of a truck. The guards emptied the water into a small basin. The basin was like a small cement pond. The guards then gave each of us a small cup. They then yelled, "Go drink!"

Imagine what happened next. Hundreds of thirsty people ran to the small basin to get a drink of water. There was pushing and shoving. Water spilled over from their cups. It was very hard to watch this fight for water. A few of us decided that we would not take part in this fight for water. We stepped aside.

We listened to what the guards were saying. They were talking about the prisoners fighting for water. The guards said, "Look at them. These are not human beings. These are not even animals. They are just small worms. They are killing each other for water!"

Worse than Being Hungry and Thirsty

It was so terrible to listen to this. I know what being hungry feels like. It is terrible. I know what it means to be thirsty. That too is terrible.

But they said we were worse than animals. They said we were worms. In their minds we were not human beings. Hearing this was worse than the hunger and thirst.

How Lucky We Are

An interesting thing happens to me since I became free. It happens when I talk or write about not having water. I get thirsty. I'm thirsty right now! This makes me want a drink of cold water in a hurry.

To this day, the best drink in the whole world is a drink of clean, cool water. Next time you are thirsty think of me. And think of how lucky we are. When we are thirsty we can almost always have a drink of clean water.

Being Counted

You might ask, "What we did all day?" After breakfast and lunch we had to line up. We lined up in columns of five. We had to stand for hours to be counted. The SS called this *Zhale Appell[24]*. Why did they count us? We were behind the electrified fences.

There were guards around us. There were guards in the watchtowers. The guards had guns. Nobody could escape.

The counting was torture for us. We were weak, hungry, thirsty, tired and sick. People fainted left and right. Those who fell were picked up. They had fainted but they were still alive. The guards threw them into waiting trucks. The trucks were soon full with bodies that were driven away. We never saw these people again.

---

[24] *Zhale Ap-pell: Roll call. During this time, all prisoners had to stand at attention.*

What did we do when we weren't standing to be counted? Nothing! Doing nothing was terrible. When it was rainy we had to sit in the mud. If it was sunny we had to sit in the dust. All the time we were hungry and thirsty. Often we would ask each other, "What is happening to us?" But many of us never gave up. We had hope that one day we would be free. Some of us became friends.

How Friends Saved My Life

We were in Auschwitz for many weeks. One morning I was feeling sick. The guards had us line up. They were counting us. I fainted. I almost fell. That would have been the end of me. But I had a "treasure." I had become friends with other prisoners. I hope all of you have friends. They are important and **precious**[25]. You can make one anywhere. In my case my friends saved my life.

I was standing in line with three of my friends. When I got dizzy and fainted they grabbed me. They watched the guards and took turns holding me up. They held me up by my dress. These dear friends risked their lives to save mine.

I was very skinny. But it must have still been hard to hold me up. When the counting was over they gently put me down. When I "came-to" they told me what happened. I was laughing and crying at the same time. I knew then, as I know now, that these three women saved my life.

Many years later I went back to Hungary. While I was there I met one of these friends. When my friend saw me she opened her arms. She asked if I still

---

[25] *Pre-cious:* Dearly loved and valuable.

remembered what happened at Auschwitz. I told her, "Of course I do.

I wouldn't be here if the three of you hadn't saved my life." We hugged. We cried. We laughed and we celebrated life!

As a survivor I have learned that celebrating life is important. What do I mean by this? I believe that we should never take for granted the fact that we are alive. Life is precious. After suffering and danger it is an extra gift to be alive.

Picture by Mary Morgan Vegdahl-Crowell, 7th grade ('02), Manson Secondary School, Manson, Washington (Used with permission)

Chapter Four

Learning the Truth, But not Giving Up

Days and weeks went by. I was missing my dear ones. What had become of my mother? What had become of my grandmother? What had become of my sister and baby brother? I wanted to know. So did some of the other prisoners in my barrack. So we decided to ask.

Finding Our Dear Ones

We were afraid of the SS guards. But we had to know. So we asked: "Where are our dear ones? Are they in another camp? Will they be coming back to our camp?" At first we got no answers. We kept on asking. Finally one day we got an answer. This is the part of the story that is hardest to tell.

One of the guards was very angry. She started to yell at us. She asked, "Do you really want to know where your family members are? Do you see above you? Do you see the dark *ash*[26] clouds? Do you smell what I smell? Do you see the fire in the chimney going on day and night?"

We answered, "Yes we do" to all of her questions. We did see the dark ash-looking clouds. Many times we choked on something. This something was some kind of ash. We did not know what the ash was made from. We did smell the terrible smell. Only we did not know what caused this. And yes, we did see the fire day and night.

---

[26] *Ash*: The black or gray powder left after something is burned.

But we didn't know what this fire was for. We answered all of the guard's questions. But still we did not know what had happened to our dear ones. We begged, "Please, please, tell us about our families. Where are they?"

The angry guard raised her arm. She pointed first to the dark, ash-looking cloud. She then moved her arm toward the chimney fire. She said: "Here are your relatives. There they go!" At first we didn't know what the guard was talking about. Maybe we didn't understand her.

Maybe we were so sick that we didn't understand the guard properly. Maybe the guard is so sick that she doesn't know what she is saying. I am sorry to tell you that the guard did know what she was saying.

Later I Learned

My dear ones went to the left. Later I learned that they had to walk down a long road. They waited like I did. They were made to undress. They were shaved. They were taken to shower room.

But they did not take a shower. There were showerheads. But the showerheads were not to be used. These were not shower rooms. They were gas chambers. The gas they used was **Zyclon B**[27]. All our dear ones died there. They choked to death on gas. Then their bodies were taken to large ovens. Their bodies were burned to ashes. That was what the fire in the chimney was for. That was what made the dark ash-looking clouds. That was what happened to all our dear ones.

---

[27] *Zy-clon B*: A deadly gas. This gas was first used for killing rats and insects. Later it was used to kill prisoners in gas chambers.

Picture by Terrence Erickson, 6th grade ('02), Acme Elementary School, Acme, Washington (Used with permission)

Terrible Pain and Sorrow

Yes, the guard told us what had happened to our families. We felt terrible pain and sorrow. I hope you never have to experience anything this painful. Now I realized what would never happen again. Never again would I hear my grandma sing.

Never again would I watch her bake her cookies. Never again would I see my mother's smile. Never again would I play with my sister. Never again would I see my baby brother. Never again!

But we were still in this terrible place. Can you imagine being forced to stay in this prison? We would never see our families again. But we still had to breathe that air. We still had to choke on the ash. We still had to smell that smell.

We, who were still alive, lost more and more weight. More and more of the prisoners fainted and were taken away in trucks.

Who is that Woman?

Many days later I was wandering outside the barracks. I was thinking, " I don't want to die. I am young. I want to live. Will somebody please come save us?"

I looked up. I could see someone looking at me. I saw her face. She looked familiar. But it was hard to tell who she was. She was a starved skeleton. She had no hair. She had a ragged dress.

Picture by Courtney Bradnt, 6th grade ('02), Acme Elementary School, Acme, Washington (Used with permission)

I was sure I had met this person before. I looked more carefully but I could not remember her name. I walked closer and closer towards the barrack. The woman walked closer to me. Then I saw who she was.

She was me! I was seeing myself in the reflection of

the barrack's window! The window was like a mirror. Can you imagine how terrible we looked? I couldn't even recognize myself.

To a Different Camp

Days went very slowly. We prisoners talked to each other. We helped each other. We tried to talk about hope and freedom.

One day an SS soldier came to camp. It was the same soldier we had seen before. He was the one with the shiny uniform pointing to the left and the right. He was the one who separated us from our dear ones. His name was **Dr. Joseph Mengele[28]**.

He was a doctor. He was supposed to heal people. He looked like a human being. But he didn't act like one. We were scared when we recognized him.

We asked each other, "Why do you think he is here?" First we tried to hide. Later we learned that he needed 1,000 prisoners to be **slave-workers[29]**.

These 1,000 prisoners would be sent to Germany. My friends and I were "**selected**"[30] to become slave-workers. The guards took us to the showers. We each got "real" prisoner's uniforms. We were put into cattle cars again. We took a long, long train ride.

---

[28] **Dr. Jo-seph Men-ge-le**: A doctor in Auschwitz. His nickname was Dr. Death. He got this name because he decided who lived and who died.

[29] **Slave-workers**: The Nazis forced prisoners to work without pay. They worked in factories. They were like slaves. They were slave workers.

[30] **Se-lec-ted**: Prisoners had to line up. Some were then sent to the gas chambers. Others were sent to a labor camp. The process by which this choice was made was called "selection."

I was sad because I was leaving without my dear ones. But I was happy to be getting out of Auschwitz. We traveled from Auschwitz, Poland to **Duchenwald**[31], Germany. We were given some bread and soup to eat.

When we finally, arrived in Germany, we were taken to a camp near the city named **Allendorf**[32]. Compared to Auschwitz, our barracks were like a "hotel." We no longer had to sleep on the floor. We had bunk beds. We even had blankets.

We were able to shower without fear that we would be killed. We were even given ten days to rest. There was a bit more food. But we were still hungry.

The Potato Skin Mystery

During these ten days, an interesting thing happened to us. One of my friends was walking near the barracks. She noticed, next to the kitchen door, a bucket full of potato skins. It was cooked potato skin. It was there to be thrown away. My friend picked up the bucket and brought it into the barracks. We had a feast! We had a whole bucket of potato skins to eat! When we were done she took the bucket back.

The next day we asked our friend to go again. Maybe there is another bucket full with potato skins. Our friend went to look. Again, there was a bucket. Again, it was full with skins. We started to eat them. This time there was more real potato on the skins. Oh, we were so happy!

---

[31] *Bu-chen wald, Ger-man-y.* One of the concentration camps in Germany.

[32] *Al-len dorf, Ger-man-y.* A small town in Germany. In this town was the slave labor camp to which Noemi was sent.

The next day we sent her out to look for the bucket. Again, there were skins. And again there was even more potato left on them. This happened every day for ten days.

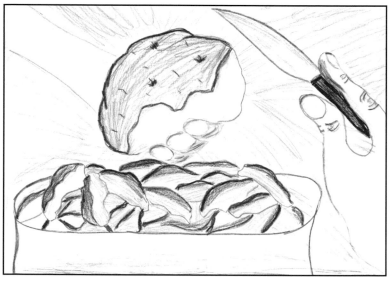

Picture by Meghan Strachila, 6th grade ('02), Acme Elementary School, Acme, Washington (Used with permission)

Later I learned

Many years later, when I was free, I learned the answer to the mystery. I met the person who put out the bucket of skins. She was also a prisoner. She worked in the kitchen. She put out the bucket and watched. She saw a skeleton of a prisoner pick up the bucket. The next day she made sure that the potato peels had skin and potato. She risked her life to help us. If she had been caught she could have been killed.

The Life of a Slave Worker

The Nazis were treating us better now. This was because they wanted us to work for them. Even the Nazis realized that people who faint easily couldn't work in a factory. Guards selected me to work with 24 other women. Each day we walked 5 miles to our workplace. It was getting cold. We had wooden shoes. But we had no jacket or socks.

The guards took us into a room. Here we found low lying tables with trays. In the trays were round colorful items and wires. Some were red, some were yellow, others were brown, black or green. We were told that these round, colorful items were *poisonous*[33].

They were not only poisonous. They were *explosives*[34]! Our job was to make parts for bombs. We were told to be very careful. If we dropped them we might all die. At first we thought we should drop them. With any luck we could kill the Nazis. But we were young. We wanted to live. We knew that an explosion could kill us too. Soon we would come up with another plan.

Sabotage!

We learned our jobs well. But the thought of making bombs did not please us. We knew that these bombs would be used against the Americans. We did not want the bombs to kill the Americans. We wanted the Americans to free us. But they could not *liberate*[35] us if the bombs we helped to make killed them.

The guards watched us carefully. Soon they saw that we had learned our job well. So the guards left us alone.

---

[33] *Poi-son-ous*: Something that can kill you or make you very sick. A poison can be breathed in the air. A poison can also hurt you by touching it or tasting it.

[34] *Ex-plo-sives*: Something that can blow up, like parts of a bomb.

[35] *Lib-er-ate*: To set free. When one army defeats the other army it liberates, or sets free, the prisoners.

The guards could only speak German. We could speak two languages: German and Hungarian. So we talked to each other in Hungarian. And we made a plan. Our plan was **sabotage**[36]. We decided that we would mix up the explosives. We would put the green part in the red space.

We would put the brown part in the black space. Then we would hook up the wires wrong. We did this when the Nazis weren't looking.

Sabotage felt so good! We were laughing and giggling about what we had done. The Nazis heard this and thought that we were happy working for them. We were proud. We hoped the bombs we made would not explode. We hoped they would not kill anyone.

Later I Learned

Many years later I was in our town's library. I was telling my story to a large group. In the group was an older man. I got to this part of the story. I told about the sabotage. The older man raised his hand. He said, "I know! I know!"

This surprised me. So I asked him, "What do you know." He said that he was in the American army at the end of the war. He said the Nazis were bombing them day and night. He said that some of the bombs fell but didn't work! These bombs couldn't kill anybody!

I smiled. I told him, jokingly, "Perhaps the bombs that didn't explode were my bombs!" We both laughed. There is no way to know whether it was one of our bombs. But it felt good to think that maybe our sabotage saved some lives.

---

[36] *Sab-o-tage*: An act against an enemy. This act damages the enemy's equipment or ruins the enemy's ability to fight.

Chapter Five:
Finally Free, Feeling Loving and Sadness

We worked, every single day, for seven months. One day we were told that we would leave the camp on the next morning. It was easy to get ready. We had nothing to pack. All we had was our prisoner outfits. The next day we had to line up. The gates were opened and everybody marched out. The guards surrounded us. They made us march down the road. We went up and down hills and through forests.

Why the Nazis Changed Their Clothes

Finally we stopped to rest for a short time. When we got up we noticed something had changed. The Nazis were not wearing their SS uniforms any more. They had changed into their *civilian*[37] clothes. The Nazis were wearing regular shirts and pants. We were surprised. But we thought this must be a good sign. The American army must be getting closer and closer. We guessed that this was why the Nazis had thrown away their uniforms. They must not have wanted the Americans to be able to tell that they were Nazis.

Stepping Out and Sneaking Away

The Nazis made us start marching again. We went down a road until we got to a Highway. We were all very tired from the marching. Some of us were getting very weak. Later I learned that this was called a

---

[37]*Ci-vil-ian:* Things that belong to citizens. Not something worn or used by people in the army.

death march[38]. The Nazis marched us away from the Americans. The Nazis wanted us to march until we were so tired that we died. We were to march until we died. This is how "death march" got its name.

While we marched my friends and I started talking to each other. We talked about escaping. We spoke in Hungarian. That way the Nazis wouldn't know what we were saying. We decided that we would "step out."

The twelve of us made a plan. One at a time, we would step into the woods. We went one at a time so the Nazis would not see the group of us gone.

It was a dangerous plan. The guards still had their guns. If they saw us they could shoot and kill us. But we wanted to be free.

When my turn came I went into the woods. I didn't look back. I got to the trees. My friends were waiting for me there. We were lucky. All twelve of us made it.

Together we ran deep into the woods. There we found a small hut made of wood. We opened the gate. It was empty. We decided to hide inside until it was safe to come out.

A Soldier Finds Us

The twelve of us, hungry and scared, hid inside the small wooden hut. Suddenly we heard footsteps. The steps were coming closer and closer. I was afraid that it was the Nazis coming to get us. I looked at my friends. They too were very frightened.

---

[38]**Death March:** A march with the purpose of making prisoners so tired that they died.

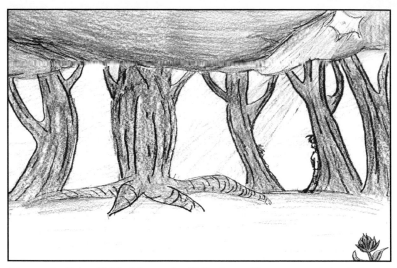

Picture by John Held, 6th grade ('02), Acme Elementary School, Acme, Washington (Used with permission)

The steps stopped right in front of the shelter. The gate was pushed open. I peeked to see who it was. It was a soldier. I read the writing on his uniform. It said, "U.S.". This soldier was an American.

The soldier asked us, "Do any of you speak English?" We shook our heads, "no." Then he asked if any of us could speak German. We said "yes." He then told us, in German, that we should not be afraid anymore.

He knew we were prisoners. He could tell by our prisoner outfits. He also saw we had very little hair. We looked like skeletons, all skin and bones.

The good soldier told us to stay in the hut. The American troops were coming closer. He warned us that we would hear gunshots and see fires. But he told us that we should not be afraid. He told us that the next day he would come back for us.

You Are Free!

As you can probably imagine, none of us could sleep that night. From our hiding place we heard gunshots. We saw fire. We couldn't wait until morning came. Later that morning the soldier came back. He looked at us and said the most beautiful sentence I have ever heard. He said, "You are free!" Then he said, "This part of Germany has surrendered!"

All twelve of us ran to the soldier. We hugged and kissed him. The poor man must have had trouble breathing. He could tell that we were hungry. He gave us chocolate, crackers and even chewing gum. We knew what to do with the chocolate and crackers. None of us had seen chewing gum before. Luckily the soldier warned us. "Don't swallow the gum."

We were free. The word for this is "liberated." The Americans set us free. We were liberated.

A Dream for the Future

The soldier took us out to the highway. The Nazis were gone! Instead there were many American soldiers. Now we were more than happy. We were thankful! Many American soldiers fought in World War II. Each of them fought so that we, all of us, you and I, and many, many other people could be free. We must always remember this.

As you know, my home was in Hungary. This is where I was born. The American soldiers set me free from the Nazis. I had a dream. I dreamed that one day I would be able to live in America. I wanted to become an American citizen. I very much hoped that my dream would come true.

Dangers in the Magic Tent

The soldier took us to the U.S.Army **Headquarters**[39]. Here soldiers asked us for our names. They asked us where our homes were.

Then they took us to the "magic tent." You may be wondering what was so magical about this tent. The answer, in just one word: FOOD!!!

The tent was a **cafeteria**[40]. Can you imagine what that smelled like to us? We had been so hungry for so long. We wanted to eat everything at once.

But first a good American doctor talked to us. He warned us. There was a great danger if we ate too much. As prisoners we had been starved. Months without food made our stomachs smaller. He told us that some people who were liberated before us did not listen. They ate too much too soon. They died from eating too much. This was a very sad thought. Imagine, finally being free but then dying from eating too much food. Although we were very hungry, my friends and I were very careful not to eat too much.

The Long Road Home

The American Army liberated me in April of 1945. In May 1945, the war was over in Europe. My friends and I were very happy. We looked forward to going home. But we had to wait four more months. This was because the many railroad tracks were destroyed during the war. It took time to rebuild the railroads.

---

[39]*Head-quar-ters*: A central place used by an army to give orders and take care of people.

[40]*Caf-e-ter-ia*: A dining area where food is served.

American soldiers helped me and my friends find a train home. The train ride took much longer than I expected. The railroads were still being repaired.

I had much time to be excited about going home. But I also had a lot of time to feel very sad. I knew I would never see my dear ones again.

My mother, my sister, my brother, and my grandmother were all ashes at Auschwitz. Who would be home when I got there?

I also knew that once we got to Budapest I would have to say good-bye to my friends. My friends would get on other trains to go to their hometowns.

I would have to say good-bye to the three women who saved my life when they held me up during Zhale Appell.

Photograph of Budapest railway station by György Pataki (Used with permission)

One week later the train arrived. I stepped off the train at Budapest. I said good-bye to my Hungarian friends. We gave each other long hugs. We cried. There I stood, alone. I was tired, lonely and numb. Where should I go? What should I do?

I Search for Family that is Alive

I knew I had an uncle and aunt who lived in Budapest. Were they still alive? If so, were they still there? My uncle was a teacher. I decided to try to find him. I would start by going to his school.

It was a long walk from the train station to my uncle's school. As I walked I felt both fear and hope in my heart. I feared that maybe my uncle was no longer alive. I hoped I was wrong.

I went to the school office. I found the school secretary. I often wonder what I looked like to her. I was wearing a dress I had made out of a red a white tablecloth. I was still very skinny. My hair was extremely short. I was dreadfully tired from the long train ride and from the long walk from the station.

I asked the secretary if my uncle was still as teacher at the school. She looked me over and asked who I was. I told her I was his niece.

The secretary stood up and shouted with joy, "YES, YES! Your uncle is here! Wait here. I will get him for you right now!" I was relieved that I had found someone.

I will never forget the look on my uncle's face when he saw me. With smiles and tears we held each other. We were so happy to see each other.

I knew what had happened to my mother, sister,

brother and grandmother. But I did not know what had happened to my father. So I asked my uncle, "Is my father alive?" My uncle's smile was even bigger now. "Yes, your father is alive."

Oh, my joy was so great! My father was alive! My uncle took me to their home where my aunt was waiting for us. I had a very happy but tearful meeting with my aunt. We told each other what had happened.

And Now the Hard Part

Some people say that surviving in the camps was the hardest part of the Holocaust. Yes, life in the camps was very hard. Millions didn't survive. I was there. I can tell you what it was like. I can tell you of the misery, the numbness and the suffering. I can tell you of the stench of death. It took everything I had to survive.

For some of us, the hardest part of the Holocaust was when we got home. No longer was fear of the Nazis at the center of our hearts. Instead the deepest sadness took over. How could I describe what happened? What words can be used to tell? How could I tell my dear father what had happened to his family? How could I tell him about what had happened to my mother who was the love of his life? How could I tell him about the death of his only son, and of my sister Elizabeth?

Even today I struggle to find words to tell you what it felt to see my father again. But I will try. My father arrived in Budapest two days later. I saw him coming up the apartment steps. My first feeling was of joy. He was alive. He survived. But he looked very different.

I gave him a big hug. As we hugged I could feel he

had lost a great deal of weight. We looked at each other. My father was always a tall man. He had excellent posture. He always stood straight. But today he seemed smaller. He was bent over.

We held each other for minutes and minutes and minutes. We were both sobbing and sobbing, terribly. Then we went into the living room and sat down.

He wanted to know the details of what happened to his family. He wanted to hear everything, from beginning to end. He wanted to know everything I knew.

I had decided, if he asked, I would tell him. So I told him everything. I told him about the cattle car. I told him about Auschwitz. I told him about the lines. I told him about the Doctor who separated us. I told him how I went to the right and our dear ones went to the left. I told him about the look in my mother's eyes as she told me to "take care." I told him how the guard pointed to the ashes in the sky and said, "There are your relatives." I told him about the gas chambers

and ashes. I told him how my friends saved my life. I told him about going to the slave labor camp. I told him about the potato peels. I told him about the sabotage. I told him about the death march and I told him how we stepped out. I told him how the Americans liberated us.

Noémi's Father

46

I told him what I have told you in this book.

We held each other. He was crying. So was I. There are no words for the pain we each felt.

Now I know how important it was for me to tell him. He needed to know. And I needed to tell. When a person feels terrible pain they must find someone they trust. I was afraid to talk about it. I was holding so much terrible pain in myself. I trusted my father and he was the first one I told. A little later I told my husband, Earnest. But, for a long time, I didn't tell anyone else. I was still afraid.

Chapter Six:
Return to Auschwitz

As you already know, I was liberated in April 1945. I got back to Budapest. I told my father what had happened in the camps. In this last part of my book, I will tell you a little about what has happened since then.

Noémi and Earnest's Wedding Photo

When I got back I found out that my boyfriend was still alive. His name was Earnest. He had been sent to a slave labor camp. When Earnest learned that I was alive he came to visit. During the visit he asked me to marry him. As you can see from the picture on the left, he was handsome. He was very smart and a teacher. He had missed me very much. We were in love with each other. So I said, "yes." We got married in October of 1945 and we were married for the 49 years that were to come.

Earnest and I had two sons, Steve and George. When George was two-years-old, I went back to college to become a teacher. Later I taught 5-8th grade boys.

In 1956 Earnest, Steve, George and I escaped from Hungary. Why we left Hungary and how we escaped is an exciting story. It would take many pages to tell, so I will not tell it now. We arrived in the United States in 1957. My dream to come to America had come true. I was very happy, tired and excited.

I worked hard and learned how to speak English. I wanted to learn the language of my new country. Soon I became a teacher in St. Louis, Missouri. I taught 6th grade for 16 years and loved it. From time to time I would tell my students about my life before the war. I told them how we escaped to America. But I didn't tell anyone about what happened in the camps. I was still afraid to tell. No longer did I wear a yellow star on my blouse, but I still wore it inside my head.

In 1984, after retiring from teaching, I started to tell my story. I started to tell it in schools and churches. It took me forty years to be able to talk about the death camps. I am a free woman now. My memories will never leave me. But I am not afraid any more.

Steve and George grew up, married and had children of their own. I am the proud grandmother of five grandchildren. My husband, Earnest, got ill in 1989. He got a sickness called **Alzheimer's**[41] disease. I was his caregiver. He died in my arms in 1994.

I Return to Auschwitz

I suffered in Auschwitz. My dear ones died there. I wanted to learn more about the fate of my dear ones. As a free woman, I wanted to go back to the place where they had died. My good friend, Ray Wolpow, wanted to

---

[41] *Al-ziem-er's dis-ease:* This is a disease that first causes a person to lose parts of his memory. Later this disease causes the person to not be able to think and speak clearly. Finally, the person becomes totally helplessness and must be cared for like a small child.

go with me. He wanted to be with me, take pictures, and write everything down.

In 1995, Ray and I met in Budapest. He was tired from a long plane ride from America. The next day Ray and I took a train to Poland. It was a long and tiresome ride.

Noémi in the taxi going to Auschwitz (1995)

The next morning we got into a taxi. The driver asked where we wanted to go. Ray answered, "Auschwitz." When I listened to this, tears came to my eyes. I had many questions and feelings at the same time.

Would I find the place where we were separated? Would I find the barrack in which I suffered? Would I find the gas chambers in which my dears ones died? I thought, "Oh my God! Today I am a free woman taking a taxi to Auschwitz. I feel so much sadness but I wanted to go very much."

Soon the driver told us that we were getting closer. I didn't recognize the road, houses, or anything. Why? The last time I was here I was in the cattlecar as a prisoner. I couldn't see anything.

We pulled into a parking lot. Everything looked different.

Auschwitz #1

Opening a Door in Auschwitz #1

Auschwitz was a very big camp. We were in the parking lot for Auschwitz #1. Here we found many brick barracks. We found a sign. Its words were written in Polish, English, French and German. They said:

YOU ARE ENTERING A PLACE OF
EXCEPTIONAL HORROR AND TRAGEDY.
PLEASE SHOW YOUR RESPECT FOR THOSE
WHO SUFFERED AND DIED HERE
BEHAVING IN A MANNER SUITABLE TO
THE DIGNITY OF THEIR MEMORY.

I stopped to think and feel my feelings. Yes, this was a place where many suffered and died. I know. I was there. I am a witness.

Many of the barracks had been made into museums. Ray and I went to the barrack that was a Hungarian museum. There were pictures and names of many of those who died and suffered. As I looked around I became sad. I started to feel the pain and I remembered the horror.

We walked around and then decided that we wanted to leave. We found a door but it would not open. Ray said, "Let's go back and find another door. This one appears to be locked." I did not agree. I told Ray that I am a free woman now. Nobody can lock me in anymore.

I went to the door and started to shake it. I turned the lock back and forth. Then I raised my foot and kicked the door really hard. The door opened. I felt so good. I was able to get out with my own strength. We stepped out into

the alley. Ray asked to take a picture of me, a "free woman in Auschwitz." I held my arms high and with my fingers made a victory sign.

Later that day, Ray and I went to the **archives**[42]. Here we found maps and papers. We found a paper with my name on it. My family and I had been in Auschwitz 2-Birkenau. We would go there next.

---

[42] *Ar-chives:* A place where records are kept. The archives at Auschwitz have records of millions who were prisoners there.

Noémi stands in front of the gates of death. (1995)

Returning to Auschwitz #2-Birkenau

When we arrived at Auschwitz #2-Birkenau I recognized where we were. This was the "Gate of Death." Ray saw me looking around.

He took pictures. I didn't pose. We didn't talk.

Noémi points to BII/C

Look at the picture above. I found a map. I found the area of my barracks. It was BII/C. Look at all the rectangles. Each rectangle was a barracks. In each rectangle were 600 people! Can you imagine?

I found the place where my family and I were separated. I could remember my dear ones looking at me. Then I found the road my dear ones were forced to walk down. Later we learned this road leads to the gas chamber #5.

When they left Auschwitz, the Nazis blew up #5 with dynamite. But the steps are still there. So are bricks, bent irons, cables and wires. I stopped.

Noémi stands inside gas chamber #5 (1995)

This was where my loved ones died. Now I knew. My heart was beating faster and faster. Tears covered my eyes. I had a feeling that I wanted to touch everything on this spot. This was where my dear ones were killed. Ray took a picture and came over to me. We started to say Kaddish. Kaddish is the old Jewish prayer said to honor those who have died. We couldn't finish saying Kaddish. We were crying.

Slowly we moved away. I noticed a black marble grave marker. On it were carved words. These words said:

> In the memory
> of the men, women, and children
> who fell victim to the Nazi *genocide*[43]
> Here lie their ashes.
> May their souls rest in peace.

Now I knew.

Finding A Heart Shaped Stone

Ray and I walked back to the railroad tracks. We were both very tired and sad. I found a place to sit down to rest.

I looked along the tracks. There was a man walking

---

[43] *Gen-o-cide:* The Nazis wanted to kill all the Jews. They wanted to kill every last one of them. After the Holocaust a new word was invented to give this kind of killing a name. "Genos" is the Greek word for race. "Cide is the Latin word for killing. Genocide is when an army tries to kill everyone who is of one kind of race. We are sad to say that the Holocaust was not the last example of genocide.

with a backpack. In his backpack was his baby son. His baby son was sleeping in the backpack. I looked at the father and his baby and said to Ray, "That baby is safe. He will not be killed." Ray looked a bit confused so I explained. "The Nazis killed all babies that entered this camp. But this baby is safe."With tears in his eyes, Ray smiled at the baby and me.

There were a lot of stones everywhere. Ray said he was going to pick one up. He wanted to take it home. The stone would help him to remember. I asked him to get a stone for me. But I did not want just any stone. I wanted the special one that I could see amongst the many. Ray finally found the one to which I was pointing.

Noémi holds her heart shaped stone for the first time.

It is a heart shaped stone. Its color is the color of ash. I still have that stone. When I hold it in my hand I feel I am holding my dear ones' hands.

Time to Leave

We walked back towards the "Gates of Death". It was getting late. We were tired. So I told Ray, "I want to leave now." I was amazed to hear myself say that. When I was a prisoner I couldn't say, "I am tired. I want to leave now." No, I couldn't because I was a prisoner. But this day I was free. I was able to leave, even Auschwitz, whenever I wanted to. Now I am free.

We got into the cab. We started to drive away. I looked back just once. The lasting memories of my dear ones were now going home with me.

Two Years Later

Two years later, in 1997, I went back to Auschwitz again. My oldest son, Steve, and his oldest daughter, Rachel, went with me. Rachel was 20 at the time. She was only one year younger than I was when I was sent to Auschwitz as a prisoner.

All of us were sad when we saw the Gate of Death.

Noémi, Steve, and Rachel in front of the "Gates of Death" at Auschwitz. (1997)

I showed them where the cattle car stopped and where I was separated from our dear ones. Steve wanted to find the barrack, in which I had been a prisoner.

I had been in section BIIC. The buildings were gone. But there were still foundations. The foundation is the bottom of the building. We walked for a long time and then Steve found a marker. In English Steve said, "This is building #24." His words in English triggered no memories. Then I said, in Hungarian, "Huszonnégy." Huszonnégy is the Hungarian word for 24. Then I said the German words for 24, "vier und zwanzig." When I said these numbers in German and Hungarian I knew. This was the place that I had been.

Noémi in front of building # 24 (1997)

Steve took a picture of me. I was standing in front of the place I had suffered as a prisoner. Once again I raised my arms and with my fingers made a "V" for victory sign.

Later we went to the place where our loved ones died, gas chamber #5. We stood and prayed. I noticed

Rachel walk away. She walked into the woods. I watched her and saw that she was bending down and picking up something.

When she came back she had a small bouquet of wild flowers. Tears were coming out of her eyes. She bent her head like one does to pray. Then she put the white flowers on top of the black marble gravestone. We cried together.

Rachel's Flowers (1997)

A Special Moment with Earnest

Steve, Rachel and I stood together. We remembered Earnest, the man who was my husband, Steve's dad, and Rachel's grandpa. I looked at this terrible place and I looked at Steve and Rachel. Then I said:

"Hitler wanted to kill all the Jews. He didn't want us to have children or grandchildren. Almost all our family was killed. I was supposed to die. But I survived. Here I stand with my son and his daughter. Life continues. This is a victory over hatred and death."

In my mind I hugged Earnest. I knew he was with us and very proud of his family.

From Suffering and Pain to Strength, Hope and Joy

I think back on what happened to me during World War II. I survived horror, terror and suffering. I was treated like an animal. I lost my dear ones. Sometimes people ask me how it is possible that I still love life so much. They ask me "How can you be so happy when you suffered so much?"

All these memories will always be with me. I survived. I am alive and free. I love life. I cherish my family. I love to teach. I am grateful for each new day.

I do not take any of these for granted. From suffering and pain can come strength, hope and joy. But all the sad memories will always be with me. This is the truth. I know, because I am a witness.

Epilogue[44]:
The Reasons Why
I Keep Telling My Story

Some people ask me, "Why do you keep telling your story?" They say, "It happened a long time ago. Doesn't it hurt to keep telling it over and over again?

You have read this book, so you know the first part of my answer: With time, fear can change to courage. The first person I told was my father. Then after I got married I told my husband, Earnest. But after that, I didn't tell anyone for a long time. I didn't tell a single soul. Why? I didn't tell anyone because I was afraid.

Never Give Up!

As a prisoner in the camps I was always in danger. I was in danger because I was a Jew. For Hitler, the fact that I was a Jew was reason enough to kill me. Do you remember the part of the story when we arrived at Auschwitz? We lined up. I was sent to the right. My dear ones went to the left. They killed my dear ones. The Nazis killed them and they killed millions of others.

Those of us who were sent to the right were still alive. But we suffered a lot. We lost weight and looked like skeletons. We were treated cruelly. We had to stand in line to be counted. If we passed out we went to the trucks.

It was hard to get over my suffering and pain. It was not easy. Even after I was liberated, that fear was still

---

[44] **E-pi-logue:** A short speech told to the reader at the end of a book.

in me. It took a great deal of time to recover. I had to be patient. I had to have hope that slowly the fear would go away. I had to remember. Never give up! With time fear can change to courage.

Believe in Yourself.

Under Hitler I had to wear a yellow star. After liberation I didn't have to wear that star any more. But it still felt like it was burning on my chest. In America, I don't have to wear a yellow star. Today I choose to wear a necklace with the Star of David.

The fear is finally gone. I tell my story so people can remember that sometimes it takes a long time to get over a great fear. I am proud of who I am. You can be proud of who you are.

Hatred is Dangerous. Remember Teasing and "Name-Calling" Hurt!

I hope that by the time you finish reading this book you will remember what happens when people hate others. Hate, **prejudice**[42] and **bigotry**[43] are wrong and dangerous. Remember, Hitler hated the Jewish people so much that he was willing to give the orders to kill them all! Do you remember the story about the

---

[45] **Pre-ju-dice:** This word comes from the "pre" and "judge." When someone judges another person before they get to know them, this is a kind of prejudice. So if someone judges all Jews, Blacks, Women, etc., without getting to know each individual person, this is prejudice.

[46] **Bi-go-try:** Bigotry is a word to describe what a bigot believes and how he acts. A bigot is a person who thinks he is completely right. A bigot feels that no one should question what he believes. A bigot believes that anyone who disagrees with him is evil or wicked.

prisoners fighting over water? The Nazis hated us so much that they thought we were less than animals!

I hope you agree with me when I say that "name-calling" is wrong and dangerous. I hope you will agree that even teasing someone at school is wrong and dangerous. "Name-calling" hurts! Teasing hurts! Doing this gives a person the feeling that there is something wrong with them. It gives them the feeling that people don't like them. I know. I was called hurtful names. I was treated like less than a human being. After Auschwitz I felt even stronger that people should not be treated that way.

Sometimes I am surprised because I hear students say that they "hate" someone. Do they really mean what they are saying? Sometimes I am asked if I hate the Nazis for what they did to my dear ones. No, I do not hate anyone. I feel pain. But I do not feel hate. When you hate someone you become a prisoner. Don't become a prisoner of your own hate.

One of my reasons for telling my story is to let it be an example. We all need to be reminded of the harm even a little hatred can do. I hope you feel that way about teasing and "name-calling" too.

Building a Memorial of Love

You know what happened to my grandma, my mother, my sister and my baby brother. The Nazis killed them the day we arrived in the camp. Their ashes are somewhere in Auschwitz. When I talk about them their memories are with me. I feel like I am sending my love to them.

Sometimes when I talk about them, I look into

the eyes of those who are listening. I can see that they are thinking about my dear ones too. This is healing. Talking about my dear ones is like building a memorial of love.

Learning a New Language and Making Your Life Better

Not everyone was born speaking English. If we want to speak English we have to learn. Some of us learned a different language first. I spoke Hungarian as a child. Later, while going to school, I learned to speak German. Being able to speak German helped me to survive in Auschwitz.

When I came to America I did not speak English. I wanted to learn the language of my new country. My husband, Earnest, and I worked hard and learned. My sons learned faster than we did. I still have an accent. My sons do not. Perhaps you are learning faster than your parents. We went to night school to learn English. My sons helped us to learn. Our English got good enough to go to an American college. We became teachers in American schools. Our sons learned English and went to college. Steve became a doctor and George became an engineer.

One of the reasons I tell my story is as an example. Learning new languages can save your life. But you are going to have to work hard and take chances. Learning new languages can help you make a wonderful life. If you are learning a new language, study hard. You have great things ahead of you.

Never Again!

There are people who say that the Holocaust didn't happen. Maybe you have heard about them. Maybe you have seen them on TV or in the newspaper? Some of them are called Neo-Nazis. Some of them are called Skinheads. They are full of hate. When I hear them say that the Holocaust didn't happen I get very angry and sad.

I would like to ask these people a question. If the Holocaust did not happen then where are my dear ones? Only my grandmother would not be alive. My mother, my sister and my brother would still be alive. My brother and sister would have children and grandchildren. So, where are they?

I know where they are. My dear ones are dead. They were killed in Auschwitz.

You have heard from me what happened at Auschwitz. We all should know and learn from what happened during WWII. We have to remember. All of us need to make sure that a Holocaust never happens again. Not to a single human being. It should never happen again.

Sharing is Healing

Why do I keep telling my story? Why? Because it is important to remember that fear can change to courage. Because it is important to believe in yourself. Because "teasing" and "name-calling" are dangerous. Because hatred is like a prison. Because I am building a memorial of love. Because it is important to learn a new language. Because what happened during the

Holocaust must never happen again. Never again, not to one single human being!

All of these are reasons. But the most important reason for telling my story is the title of this book: *Sharing is Healing.* When I tell my story I look into the eyes of the people who are listening to me. I see respect, sympathy and love. Seeing this is healing. The pain is still there. But each time I see the respect, sympathy and love in their eyes, the pain gets less and less.

I hope that if you have sadness in your heart that you will find someone you can trust to tell. I hope they will listen with respect and love. Doing this has made my life better. It helped me to share my memories with you. If something terrible happens to you, I hope someone will listen. I am not afraid anymore, but the pain is still there.

Good-bye For Now

It's time to say good-bye. I hope that some day you and I will meet. Perhaps we will give each other hugs. Good-bye for now. Take good care of yourself. And thank you for listening.

Why and For How Long?
Afterward to the 2nd Edition

Having read this book, you know that all my dear ones, except my father, died in Auschwitz. From chapter five, you know that after I got home I had a very hard job. I had to tell my father what had happened to Nina my grandmother. I had to tell him what happened to my mother, his dearest Juliska. I had to tell him what had happened to my sister, his beloved daughter, Elizabeth. I had to tell him what had happened to his son, my baby-brother Gabor. I had to tell him what I had to do to survive. I had to tell him what it was like to smell the smoke and choke on the ashes.

You know I had promised myself that if he asked, I would tell him it all. We cried in each other's arms for a long time. We wept, and I told him. I now realize that at that time, it was almost life-saving for me to tell him. I was holding such terrible pain in myself. I told him it all. It was painful, but it was healing. In my father's arms I learned that sharing is healing.

I continue to tell this story, but my father was the first person I told. For this reason I wish to tell just a little bit more about my father. He suffered greatly. He kept a **_diary_**[47] while he was waiting for us. Writing about his pain in this diary helped him to survive. Let me tell you how.

---

[47] **_Diary_.** A special book in which people can write about their feelings. People also use a diary to write about what is happening each day. My father used an empty appointment book to write in. He wrote in his diary every day.

Why My Father Decided to Keep a Diary

At the end of the war, my father returned to our town. He went to the place that had once been our home. Our house was gone. It had been destroyed by bombs. He looked through the rubble of what had once been our home. He found some pictures and a small appointment book. But he did not find us. He looked everywhere for us. Later he learned that we had all been sent to Auschwitz.

Had any of us survived? My father could not find an answer. How horrible this must have been for him. Were we dead or alive? How had we suffered? Would we ever come home? He missed us and wanted to know. Just thinking about this brings tears to my eyes. Oh, how he wanted to know!

While he was waiting, my father decided he would keep a diary. This way he would have a way to release some of his most painful thoughts. He decided to write in the small appointment book he found. Every day he wrote in his diary. Many of the pages have tear stains from his crying as he wrote.

My father used an empty appointment book for his diary.

A Safety Valve

Let me tell you a little about what he wrote. On the first few pages my father compares his head to a *"boiler building up steam."* His feelings are the steam. They are boiling inside of him. This steam gets worse when he imagines the deadly gas of Auschwitz. He says that he is using his diary as a *"safety valve,"* so that *"he will not explode."* He has no idea how many of us, if any, have survived.

My father was so sad that he wasn't taking care of himself. He couldn't sleep and he didn't want to eat. How could he? Were we alive or dead? He wrote:

My friends are reminding me that I look terrible. They remind me that I should take care of myself, because if all of you come back I will be gone. But how can I do that? ...How can you say to a river to change its course and flow backwards?...

*Are you alive? I don't know? Who is among you that I might see again?... **Why, and for how long?**... How terrible it is just to write this down.*

The Poem Named "Why and For How Long?"

"Why and for how long?" This cry came from my father twice in his long life. The first time was when he was a young man. He had been a soldier in the Hungarian Army during World War I. He was captured and sent to a prisoner of war camp. The camp was far away, in a place called **Siberia**[48]. While he was there he wrote a poem to his girlfriend, Juliska. She was waiting for him back in Hungary. They were in love and planned to get married. The poem expressed his love and longing. It also expressed his suffering and hope.

---

[48] **Siberia**: A region in the eastern part of Russia. It is many hundreds of miles away from Hungary.

"Why and for how long?" This cry came a second time. This time it was after World War II. My father was no longer a young man. He had just come back from the forced labor camp. He was a husband and a father who hadn't seen his family in a long time. But where was his family? They had been sent to Auschwitz. Would he ever see them again?

Tears stained the pages of my father's dairy.

My father sat down to write in his diary. On the Jewish calendar the day was ***Tisha B'Av***[49], a Jewish day of mourning. My father wrote that he found it hard to mourn for the Temple. He himself was feeling such great pain and suffering. This pain was made worse because he didn't know if his family was even alive. He didn't know what had happened to us. How long must he wait? This question reminded him of the poem he wrote during World War I: *Why and For How Long?* Here is what he wrote:

---

[49] ***Tisha B'Av***: Hebrew for the 9th day of the Jewish calendar month of Av. On this day many Jews remember the destruction of the first and second Temples in Jerusalem. The first temple in Jerusalem was destroyed by the Babylonians on the 9th of Av in 586 B.C.E., and the second by the Romans on the 9th of Av in 70 C.E.

70

*I wrote this poem in Siberia.... Small parts of it
are in my mind as I wait for you. This afternoon
I was able to recall the whole poem... as I wrote
I clearly visualized you and our future together.
But today these words have even more meaning.
Can I dream of our future again? Are you alive?
Without you what will I do?*

Why? And for How Long?

*Do you know?
You the beauty of my world,
Do you feel it?
You the most beautiful on this earth,
Why? The **yearning**[50] hurts, it is burning.
Why? And for how long?*

*Did you notice, dear soul?
Did you comprehend, you, the wish of my heart?
Do you feel the hope, my yearning?
Why? And for how long?*

*I will always wait for you
My yearning is limitless
Where is the end of my sorrow?
Why? And for how long?*

*On the wings of my yearning
I fly towards you
But to arrive, to get to you
I have not the strength any more
Maybe you have forgotten me?
Why? And for how long?*

*My soul is tired
My body is weak
I am standing at the edge of my grave
My grave is waiting for me with its Peace
Without you, why would I want to live?
Why? And for how long?*

---

[50] **Yearning.** Yearning is a feeling. It is the feeling of really missing someone.

71

You know the rest of this story. His wait ended when I came home. I told him that his sweet Juliska, my sister and my baby brother had all been killed.

Sharing and Healing with Reading and Writing

I have my father's diary because he gave it to me before I moved to the United States. At that time he asked that I not read it right away. Instead he thought I should *"save it for some quiet reading moments."*

Before the Holocaust, my family had many "quiet reading moments." In his diary he remembered these. On August 14, 1945, while still waiting for us he wrote:

> *Every night I dream about what has happened to you. I can find comfort only in remembering. I remember seeing Anyu at the Sabbath table. She is reading in a very quiet atmosphere after dinner. And then, Noemi, I see you sitting opposite me. While you read, you comb your hair. I also see little Elizabeth sitting next to you. We are family, and we are very much in love as we do our reading.*

Even today, 60 years later, these words bring the whole picture back to me. Before we lit the candles each of us was deep in our own world. But after the blessings and our meal, we sat together and read. This was a time of quiet, shared enjoyment and love. We sat together. We honored each other's privacy, and we read. There was strength, a unity, a harmony.

We were not alone. It was more than a routine.

It was a celebration. It was a quiet way to show love and to enjoy each other. Even in the most terrible times, my father would remember who sat where...and I remember it too. Whether or not you have a great sadness in your heart, I wish for you the blessing of reading and writing together with those you love. Take the time to enjoy each other's love in this way.

If you have a great sadness in your heart, I have a suggestion and a wish for you. No matter how great the pain, you might find healing by writing it down. Keeping a diary helped my father every day until I came home. Even today, his diary is a blessing to me, to my children and my grandchildren. You don't have to write. But if you do, your words, read someday by others, might be healing.

Maybe you will write about your sadness. Maybe you will not. Either way, I have a wish for you. May you find someone you trust to share your story. May they listen with love and respect. This kind of sharing is healing. I know. I'm a survivor. I am a witness and I love life.

My Hope

I am a survivor and a witness. I love life. I have learned that healing can be found in listening, believing, and remembering with love. You may have a horrific memory. You may have a haunting feeling. Then again, you might not. Either way, I hope that if you are asked to listen to someone, you will do this with love. Love and respect can be given freely. When we do this, together, we make the strength to go on. Then there is hope. That is why sharing is healing.

Thank you, Ray

Many years ago, Ray Wolpow came to my house. He wanted to ask me questions. He was a teacher. Many of his students didn't like to read. He was collecting stories that explained why reading might be important to them. I was a Holocaust survivor. Ray thought my answers would be important for his students. The more I told him, the more questions he asked.

A few years later Ray went to school to become a professor. While he was in school he wrote a book. It explains why reading and writing can be important to people who have had terrible things happen to them. He tells me that my story was an important part of that book.

In 1995, I went back to Auschwitz. Ray came with me to give support in my journey. He also took pictures and tape-recorded my every sentence. He suffered with me as I went through pain and discovery. His kind support and silent understanding helped me to survive my return to Auschwitz.

When we got back we talked to many groups of students about what had happened. Ray shared a little. But mostly he listened. We made a video of one of our talks. Ray also wrote some articles for teachers to help them teach about the Holocaust.

In 2001 Ray came to me with an idea. He said that there were hundreds of books written by Holocaust survivors. Most of them were written for adults. His idea was that I write my story so younger readers could understand it. As you can see, I liked his idea.

If you look at the cover of this book you will see that I wrote this book with Ray Wolpow. Let me explain what this means. Some people say that you really don't understand something unless you can say it in simple words.

Ray and I agreed that any student could understand my story as long as we paid attention to four things:

1) In a book, students could not see me speak. They could not hear my voice. So I had to choose my words with great care.

2) Longer words and sentences are hard for some students to read. So I had to write sentences that all students could read it.

3) My story has many new words for students to learn. So I had to define new words for students in a way that would make it easy for them to learn.

4) There were many facts, feelings and ideas to share. There were also many parts to my story. I had to organize the chapters and headings so that they helped the reader understand the story.

Ray edited each chapter and helped me find the best words. We sat together for many long hours and talked about each sentence. Ray helped me organize and choose headings. This is what I mean when I say I wrote this book with Ray Wolpow.

So I am writing this to thank Ray Wolpow. If you ask Ray, he will tell you that he learned a lot from me. I am writing to thank Ray for what I learned from him. Ray is a good listener. He is a good editor. He is a good teacher. But most important, he is a good friend.

Noémi Ban